IMAGES
OF BRITAIN

Jacket: *Leeds Castle near Maidstone in Kent, 'the loveliest castle in the world'*
Jacket (back): *Hillier Arboretum near Romsey in Hampshire is the largest collection of trees and shrubs of its kind in Britain*
Half-title: *Keeping the hedges trim at Bowood House, near Calne in Wiltshire*
Title page: *Desolate waterfalls at the Pass of Glencoe, on the border of Highland and Strathclyde regions*
Contents page: *Detail from the roof of the nave at Peterborough Cathedral*
Introduction: *Ruined Llanstephan Castle, near Laugharne in Dyfed*

©The Automobile Association, 1990

This edition is published by Longmeadow Press, 201 High Ridge Road, Stamford, CT 06904

ISBN 0-681-41013-2

0 9 8 7 6 5 4 3

Typesetting by Microset Graphics Ltd., Basingstoke, Hampshire
Repro by Scantrans Pte Ltd., Singapore
Printed by Graficromo SA, Spain

Produced by the Publishing Division of
The Automobile Association

All pictures are taken from the AA Photographic Library
Written by Richard Cavendish

IMAGES
OF BRITAIN

Longmeadow Press

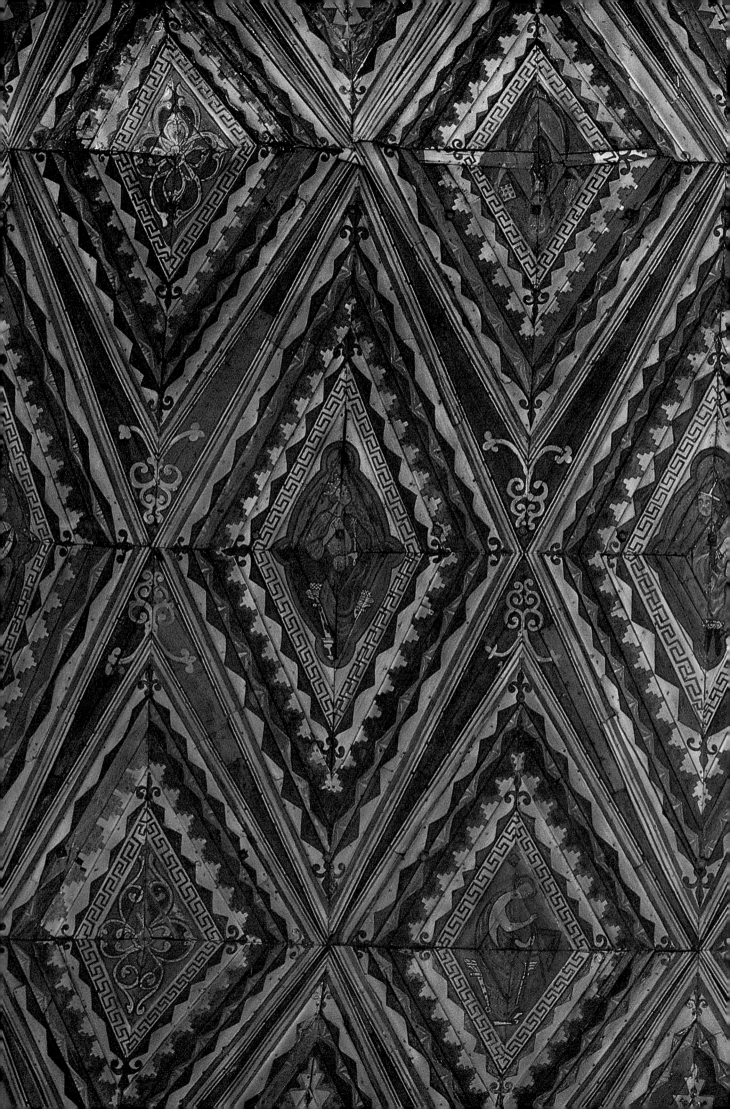

CONTENTS

INTRODUCTION

*B*efore the time of Christ, Greek and Roman geographers wrote of the 'Pretanic' or 'Britannic' islands in the northern sea. They were using the ancient Celtic name for the British Isles, which has survived in Welsh as *Prydain*. When the Romans conquered England, it became the Roman province of Britannia. The Anglo-Saxons overran the province in the 6th century, while native Britons retained their independence in Wales and Scotland. Later invaders were the Danes and the Norse, the Scots and the Normans. In the 13th century a king of England, Edward I, annexed Wales. In the seventeenth, a king of Scots, James VI, became King James I of England and Wales, uniting the thrones of the three nations. Since then, England, Wales and Scotland, each with their richly diverse heritage, have been a single unit: Britain.

*B*ritain has a remarkable variety of scenery – a variety which is mirrored in this book. A line drawn from the mouth of the River Tees on the North Sea coast, to the mouth of the River Exe in South Devon, separates the country very roughly into a highland and a lowland zone. To the north and west lie the high and solitary scenic splendours of the Welsh mountains, the Pennine Chain and the Scottish Highlands. South and east of the line are gentler, rolling areas of downland and green fields, the 'traditional' English farming countryside which is really a man-made creation of the last 250 years. Both types of landscape enrich this book.

*G*eological factors of titanic antiquity underlie, literally, both the highland and the lowland countryside of Britain. Yet almost the whole British landscape has been altered by the activities of man since prehistoric times – through farming, mining, industry and transport. This book reflects not only the grandeur of Britain's natural landscape, but also the human additions to the scene: from cottages and farms to stately mansions; from dovecots and windmills to castles and churches; from gardens to canals, railways and bridges; from a Bedfordshire brickworks to a Blackpool tower; from Kentish oast-houses to a giant waterwheel; from the rough-hewn prehistoric majesty of Stonehenge, to a Barbara Hepworth sculpture.

*T*his book is a celebration of Britain in pictures. It has separate sections on England, Scotland and Wales, and within them pictures appear by county. The shires were an English invention, which the Normans adopted. As this book makes its progress through them, from Avon to Yorkshire, from the Borders to the Scottish Islands, and from Clwyd to Powys, the natural and human diversity of Britain is tellingly revealed.

ENGLAND

Previous page *The idyllic village of Castle Coombe in Wiltshire was named the Prettiest Village in England in 1962. Houses angle down the hill to the bridge over the brook. Castle Coombe had a prosperous cloth industry at one time, and there is a story that the blanket was invented in the village by two brothers named Blanket.*

Below *The cottages at Blaise Hamlet, on the outskirts of Bristol, were designed for retired estate workers by John Nash in 1811, at the height of a fashion for these picturesque retreats. They were far more self-consciously rustic than any real country cottage.*

Above *Designed by the great engineer Isambard Kingdom Brunel, the Clifton Suspension Bridge, soaring across the gorge of the River Avon at Bristol, was completed in 1864 after his death, as a tribute to him.*

Left *In sight of the suspension bridge is another of Brunel's achievements, the epoch-making ship* Great Britain, *the world's first ocean-going, screw-propeller iron ship. She made her maiden voyage across the Atlantic in 1843, and is being restored in the Bristol dock where she was built.*

Overleaf *Bath Abbey, shining in the floodlights, was mainly built in the 16th century. It has a formidable central tower and flying buttresses. The fine west window is flanked by turrets carved with angels climbing ladders to heaven.*

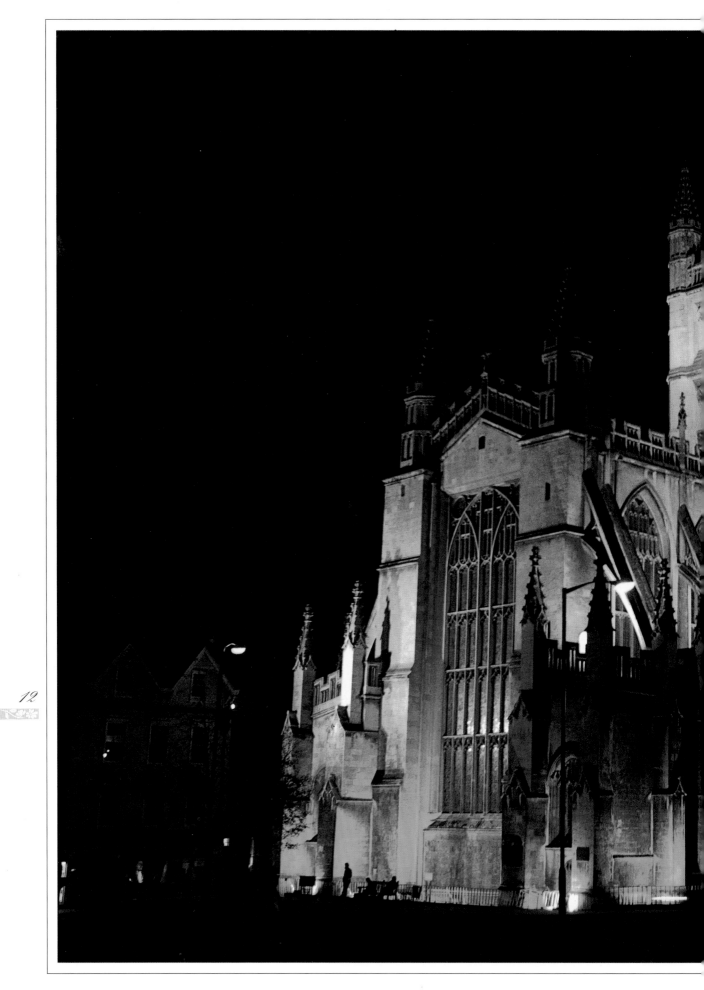

12

Right *Advertisement for mineral waters manufactured by a Bath firm which was also a brass foundry and engineering workshop. It is now preserved as 'Mr Bowler's Business' in Bath. In almost a hundred years nothing was thrown away and the cluttered premises are now a nostalgic delight.*

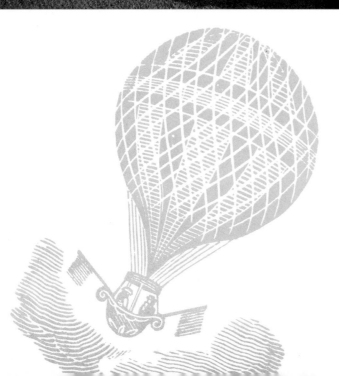

Above *A 20th-century balloon intrudes on the measured elegance of the Royal Crescent (1767-75), a monument to an age when fashionable society flocked to Bath to take the waters.*

Right *The Roman baths, with Bath Abbey in the background. The Romans were attracted to Bath by the hot springs, and built an extensive bath complex and a temple to the goddess of the springs here. The statue, right, is a 19th-century addition.*

Above *Tumbled products of the world's largest brickworks, at Stewartby in Bedfordshire, whose tall chimneys rise in the background. The county has been famous for its brick since the 15th century.*

16

Right *There are nesting boxes for 1,500 pigeons inside the stone dovecote at Willington. It was built in the 16th century, when pigeons provided fresh meat in the winter, and is now owned by the National Trust.*

Left *A modern window by John Piper in the church of St Giles at Totternhoe, a village below the northern Chiltern Hills. The rock quarried here, called Totternhoe stone, was in great demand for churches and other important buildings in the Middle Ages.*

Below *The giant airship hangars at Cardington, just outside Bedford, stand 180ft (55m) high and are 812ft (248m) long. One of them was built in 1917 to hold the R101 airship, which crashed in 1930. The other was added in 1928.*

17

Right *The largest inhabited castle in the world looms up above the boats on the Thames at Windsor. William the Conqueror founded Windsor Castle, and it has been a royal residence ever since. Its majestic appearance today is largely due to extensive rebuilding during the early 19th century.*

Below *Stanley Spencer's painting,* Christ Preaching at Cookham Regatta, *hangs in the memorial gallery to the artist in the attractive village of Cookham-on-Thames, where he was born, where he lived and which he frequently painted. The gallery is in the Methodist chapel to which he went as a boy.*

Left *'Sweet Thames, run softly till I end my song...' Scene on the river at the charming village of Sonning. This stretch of the Thames, between Reading and Maidenhead, is today one of the most heavily frequented.*

Right *High above the village of Brill, on a solitary limestone hill, rise the sails of the windmill. The weather-boarded post mill dates from 1668 and was used until 1916.*

20

Right *Benjamin Disraeli moved into Hughenden Manor in 1847, and lived there for the rest of his life. He resigned as Prime Minister in 1880, died the following year and was buried in the nearby churchyard, next to his wife. The house, now owned by the National Trust, has changed little since his time.*

Left *The Bodger's Hut, an exhibit in the Chair Museum at High Wycombe. The bodgers worked in the Chiltern beechwoods, selecting and shaping wood for the manufacture of 'Windsor' chairs, which was long a flourishing industry in this neighbourhood.*

Below *At Duxford Airfield, a former Battle of Britain fighter station, the Imperial War Museum displays its substantial collection of historic aircraft, as well as tanks, other military vehicles and naval exhibits.*

Below *Ely Cathedral rises in majesty above the surrounding fenland, which was once a tangle of almost impenetrable marshes, before it was tamed by drainage. The beautiful church took four-and-a-half centuries to build.*

Above *The National Trust owns Wimpole Hall, with its superbly civilised 18th-century interiors. It was long the Cambridgeshire seat of the Yorke family, whose grandiose monuments can be seen in the nearby church.*

Overleaf *King's College Chapel, Cambridge, is one of the supreme glories of English architecture. Wordsworth wrote in praise of its astonishing early 16th-century fan vaulting, 'scooped into ten thousand cells, where light and shade repose, where music dwells lingering – and wandering on as loth to die.'*

Right *Fishing was the main occupation of the Channel Islands before the days of tourism and the export of knitted sweaters. St Peter wears a Guernsey fisherman's sweater as he hauls in the nets in this stained-glass window, in the church at Vale on the north of the island.*

Above *Splendidly floodlit,
Mont Orgueil Castle dominates
its headland on Jersey's east
coast. In the mid-15th century
the castle was captured by the
French, but after a few years it
was retaken by an English
force. During the Civil War in
the 17th century it was held
for the Royalists.*

Above *On the small island of
Sark, noted for its precipitous
and impressive coast, the
harbour of Creux can only be
reached from the land by two
tunnels, one built in 1588 and
the other some 300 years later.*

Right *Leaning perilously at all angles, Little Moreton Hall, near Congleton, is one of the most spectacular of Cheshire's rich heritage of black-and-white, half-timbered houses. Built in the 15th and 16th centuries, it is now owned by the National Trust.*

Below *A tranquil scene on the Shropshire Union Canal near Beeston. The canal was built to link Birmingham and the industrial Midlands with the River Mersey and is now a particularly popular holiday waterway.*

28

Right *Making corn dollies at Siddington in Cheshire, a craft which has been revived in recent years. Made from the last stalks of wheat to be reaped at harvest time, the corn dolly was revered as a representative of the corn spirit.*

Opposite page *The former lifeboat house at Polpeor Cove, on a stretch of coast which has claimed many wrecks. Lizard Point, in the distance, is the most southerly spot on the English coast.*

Left *The engine house and chimney stack of an abandoned tin mine, silhouetted against the evening sky near St Just on the Land's End peninsula. Evening set in for the tin-mining industry in the 1980s. By the end of the decade, only three pits were operating.*

Above *The fish market at Newlyn, which is now the principal fishing port in Cornwall. Pilchards were once the staple catch in Cornish waters, but mackerel fishing is now more important.*

Overleaf *Fishing boats on the rippling water of the harbour at Mevagissey on the South Cornish coast. Pilchard fishing and smuggling, which were the principal occupations here up to the early 19th century, have been replaced by tourism as the main source of income.*

34

Above *A paradise of mountain scenery and magical light, the Lake District began to draw admiring visitors in the 18th century. Here the Langdale Pikes tower up beyond Langdale, a magnet for fell walkers and climbers.*

Right *Levens Hall, near Kendal, is a fine Elizabethan house, known specially for the topiary work in its gardens and its collection of working models of steam engines, showing how steam power developed in the hundred years after 1820.*

HAL BAGOT
LEVENS HALL
KENDAL

Above *Looking across lonely Wast Water in the heart of the Lake District. Three miles (1.86km) long, the lake lies in a hollow 258ft (79m) deep, scooped out by the action of an Ice Age glacier.*

Left *Looking towards the head of Longsleddale, a valley north of Kendal. The sheep, the scattered farmsteads and the brooding fells are typical of this remote and surpassingly beautiful part of England.*

Right *Glittering Derwent Water, looking heart-rendingly romantic on an overcast day. Three miles (1.86km) long and a mile (0.62km) across, studded with islands, it has been described as the loveliest lake in England. Comparatively shallow, it freezes rapidly in winter.*

Below *Tarn Hows, perhaps the most celebrated beauty spot in the Lake District, is protected today by the National Trust. Pressure to preserve the whole area from destructive development culminated after the Second World War with the establishment of the Lake District National Park.*

Left *The steamer 'Lady of the Lake' started plying on Ullswater in 1877. Second in size only to Windermere, Ullswater is another candidate for the title of the loveliest of the Lake District's stretches of water – very few of which, incidentally, are called lakes. It was on the north shore of Ullswater that Wordsworth saw the 'host of golden daffodils' which inspired his famous poem.*

Above *The opera house in Buxton was designed by the great Edwardian theatre architect Frank Matcham and opened in 1903. Opulently restored in recent years, it is the centrepiece of the town's annual opera festival.*

Right *The Monsal Dale railway viaduct is the highlight of a delightful walk along the valley of the River Wye east of Buxton, through Miller's Dale and Monsal Dale.*

Left *The Duke of Devonshire's stately mansion, Chatsworth House, gazes commandingly across the River Derwent. Completed in 1707, it houses a treasure of art and books, and the complicated waterworks in the grounds are particularly celebrated.*

Left *The Peak District has been called 'the last knobbly vertebra on the backbone of England', at the southern end of the Pennines. The national park was established in 1950. This landscape is the White Peak area. Here, gentle green fields are sheltered by towering grey walls of limestone.*

41

Above *Drystone walls are a traditional feature of the Peak District landscape. This scene is in the remote upper valley of the River Dove, east of Longnor, near the earthwork called Pilsbury Castle.*

Below *With its long stretches of coast and numerous harbours, Devon has a strong sea-faring tradition. This cottage on the harbour front at Teignmouth in South Devon is entered and left through a boat.*

Below *Outsize cooking implements and a clutter of bygones recall life as it was lived in the past, in the museum at Lynton in North Devon, where the West Lyn River swoops down from the heights of Exmoor and plunges to the sea.*

Above *Boats on the foreshore at Sidmouth on the South Devon coast, where the River Sid struggles to reach the sea. There are handsome Regency houses and terraces in the town, where Queen Victoria's parents took her for a time as a baby.*

Left *Thatchers at work on a house in Colebrooke in the centre of Devon. This is another old traditional craft which has revived in recent years, with a new appreciation of its practical advantages as well as its appearance.*

43

Overleaf *The rocks of Hound Tor, near the eastern edge of Dartmoor, a granite outcrop carved by aeons of wind and weather. The Tor's name has nothing to do with* The Hound of the Baskervilles, *though on a dark day the scenery is eerily reminiscent of the Sherlock Holmes story.*

47

Above *The East Lyn River is joined at Watersmeet by two lesser streams, Farley Water and Hoaroak Water. The river cascades over the grey Exmoor rocks between ferns and bushes.*

Left *Deep in the heart of Exmoor, the primitive packhorse bridge called Tarr Steps crosses the River Barle. How old the bridge is, no one knows, but the stones have been washed away by floods more than once, and the crossing rebuilt. It is about 180ft (54.8m) long.*

Opposite page *The abbey church at Sherborne, built in Ham stone and famed for its delectable fan vaulting. Two kings of Wessex were buried here in the 9th century. The abbey was dissolved in 1539, and the building became the parish church a year later.*

Left *Rustic bridge in the luxuriant gardens of Compton Acres at Canford Cliffs, near Poole. They were planned in 1914 as a succession of separate gardens enclosed by walls and hedges.*

49

Left *Chalky outcrops on the foreshore at West Bay, Bridport, looking west towards the National Trust's beautiful coastal estate of Golden Cap, with the highest cliff on the south coast of England.*

Below *The Black Staircase in Durham Castle. Installed by John Cosin, Bishop of Durham in 1662, and rising four storeys, it is made of black oak with carved panels of willow. The Castle, a former fortress of the Prince-Bishops, is now part of Durham University.*

Right *Ruined Barnard Castle 'standeth sweetly upon Tees', as a Tudor author wrote. The stronghold of the Balliol family in the Middle Ages and subsequently of the Beauchamps, Earls of Warwick, it is cared for today by English Heritage.*

Above *England's most spectacularly placed cathedral crowns its great rock in the horseshoe bend of the River Wear. Containing the shrine of St Cuthbert, the massive Norman church at Durham was begun in 1093 and took only 40 years to build.*

Above *Now ruined, the priory church of St Botolph's in Colchester was built about 1100. Much Roman brick was used in the construction, for Colchester had been one of the principal Roman towns in Britain from the 1st century* AD.

Right *Thatched cottages at Pleshey, north-west of Chelmsford. The scene is peaceful enough, but this was once an embattled place. The village is ringed by Norman earthwork fortifications, and there is also the mound and moat of a castle.*

Opposite page *A dozen miles or so from London, Epping Forest is the remains of a much larger royal hunting preserve. Saved from building development with difficulty in the mid-19th century, it now belongs to the City of London and encloses miles of delightful walks and bridlepaths.*

Right *Cirencester Park, a handsome 18th-century mansion with fine, wooded grounds, seen from the tower of Cirencester's parish church, which is one of the largest in England. The shielding yew hedge, 40ft (12.1m) tall, was planted in 1818.*

54

Left *The fan vaulting in the cloister of Gloucester Cathedral is among the earliest in the country, and it is possible that fan vaulting was actually invented here when the church was rebuilt in the 14th century. It was then the abbey church of the Benedictine monastery of St Peter.*

55

Left *Cotswold stone cottages by the stream in the picturesque, if violently named, village of Lower Slaughter. A whole series of little bridges cross the stream, which is a tributary of the River Dickler.*

Overleaf *One of the oldest and largest trees in the New Forest, the famous Knighton Oak is reached off the Bolderwood Ornamental Drive, north of the A35 in Hampshire. The New Forest is a former royal hunting ground, created by William the Conqueror.*

57

58

Left *On Trafalgar Day in the Royal Naval Dockyard in Portsmouth, Nelson's flagship HMS* Victory *flies the admiral's famous signal: 'England expects that every man will do his duty.' The battle resulted in an overwhelming defeat for the French and Spanish fleets, but Nelson was killed, struck down on his quarterdeck by a bullet from an enemy sharpshooter.*

Opposite page *Down below Butser Hill in the Queen Elizabeth Country Park near Petersfield, the Ancient Farm Research Project probes the past by farming as nearly as possible in the manner of the Iron Age, 2,000 years ago.*

Above *In legend, Winchester is identified as Camelot, the capital city of King Arthur and his heroic knights of the Round Table. The Round Table which hangs in the Great Hall of Winchester Castle today may have been made in the 15th century when Edward III contemplated founding a new Arthurian order of chivalry. The Gothic lettering with the names of the knights was added in Tudor times.*

Below *Sunlight sparkles on the winter snow at the simple little church of St Peter's, Rowlstone, in a remote area of Hereford and Worcester close to the Welsh border. The village lies at the southern end of the famous Golden Valley of the River Dore, loved for its tranquil beauty.*

Right *Sweeping view over the River Wye, from the celebrated beauty spot of Symond's Yat Rock, which rises sharply above a loop in the meandering river. This was already a famous view in the 18th century, when tourists came down the river in boatloads before clambering up the hill to exclaim over the prospect.*

60

Right *Megaphone at the ready, Mr Lindsay Hayes, who built the Jubilee Maze at Symond's Yat with his brother, is always ready to intervene if anyone becomes hopelessly lost in its complexities.*

62

Previous page *England's green and pleasant land: view at evening from Fromes Hill, towards the southern end of the Malvern Hills. The range, about 8 miles (12.8km) long, has links with both the author of* Piers Plowman *and the composer, Elgar.*

Above *The study at Knebworth House near Stevenage, home of the Victorian MP and popular writer Edward Bulwer-Lytton, author of* The Last Days of Pompeii *and other best-sellers. The picture above the fireplace depicts him at work in the room. He inherited the Knebworth estate and had the house romantically Gothicised.*

Left *St Albans Cathedral, built on the hilltop above the River Ver where St Alban, Britain's first Christian martyr, was beheaded. The abbey, founded in his memory in* AD 793, *became one of the richest in England. The church, which was constructed partly of Roman bricks from the city of* Verulamium, *did not become a cathedral until 1877.*

Right *The lighthouse at Withernsea, Humberside, gazing out over the grey North Sea from the eastern shore of Holderness, the long flat peninsula which runs down the eastern side of the Humber estuary to end at Spurn Head. The land here is seldom more than 30ft (9.1m) above sea level, and the sea is steadily encroaching on the coastline.*

Above *A reminder of a brighter past in the docks at Grimsby. Its closeness to the fishing grounds on the Dogger Bank made Grimsby Britain's premier fishing port in the 19th century, but its importance has declined in recent years.*

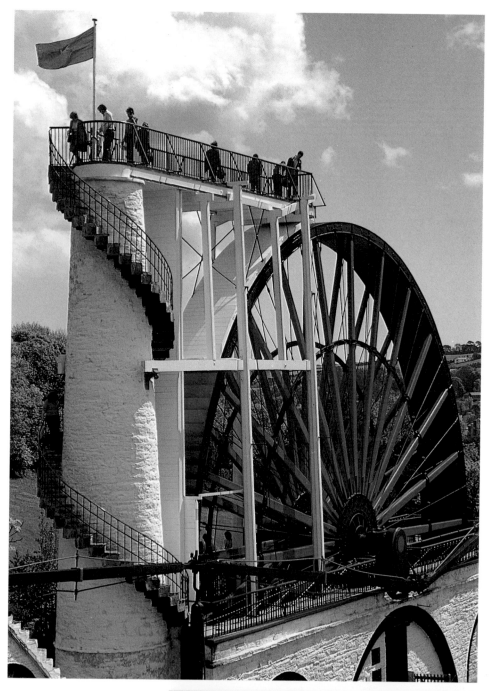

Left *The monster wheel called Lady Isabella, used to drain a lead mine at Laxey, is 72½ ft (22m) in diameter and one of the sights of the Isle of Man. With 168 buckets, it is the largest surviving waterwheel in the country. Rated at 200hp, it first turned in 1854 and worked until the mine closed in 1919.*

Opposite page *The sharp chalk spikes of the Needles, the most celebrated landmark on the Isle of Wight, jut out from the western end of the island. The lighthouse was built at the seaward end in 1858. To the right are the waters of the Solent, one of the world's most active shipping lanes, with vessels bound for, or leaving, Southampton.*

Right *The Isle of Man is probably best known for its motorcycle races, staged there since 1905, when motorbikes looked quite different. The international Tourist Trophy (TT) races, which began in 1907, are the most famous of all motorcycle events and attract visitors in droves.*

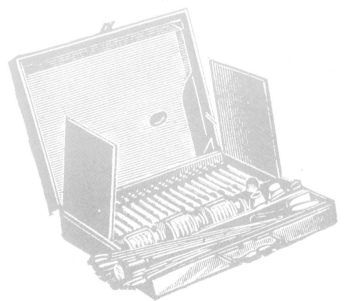

Above *Scene at Freshwater Bay on the Isle of Wight, with Stag Rock and Tennyson Down, which is named after the poet. He lived at Farringford nearby and liked to walk on the down, where he said the air was worth sixpence a pint.*

Left *Inside Yafford Mill, with restored machinery in working order. This 19th-century watermill near Shorwell has a collection of rare-breed animals and farm implements, as well as seals and waterfowl.*

Above *Picking plums at Lynsted, near Sittingbourne. Kent's reputation as 'the Garden of England' depends on its extensive fruit orchards, and the county's prevailing climate of mild winters and sunny summers helps to produce healthy yields.*

Right *Oast houses at Chiddingstone Causeway, near Tunbridge Wells. These buildings were kilns for drying hops, constructed of brick with a cowl on top, pivoted so that the opening faced away from the wind. It might take nine or 10 hours to dry a load of hops over a coal fire inside the kiln. Many oast houses have been converted into smart houses today.*

Right *The hump of Pendle Hill in the distance, seen from the north. The limestone hill stands 1,831ft (558m) high in the old Forest of Pendle, though little forest is left. It has sinister connections with groups of witches in the area: nine of them were executed at Lancaster in 1612.*

Left *Blackpool Tower in all its floodlit glory. Standing 520ft (158m) high, and modelled on the Eiffel Tower in Paris, it was built in the 1890s. Every autumn thousands of light bulbs are switched on for the famous Illuminations all along the front. In 1840 all that stood here was a row of houses.*

Right *The Shire Hall in Lancaster was built in 1796. It was designed as an extension of the town's historic castle, in the Gothic style. Inside there are ornate stone canopies and Gothic furnishings.*

Left *Fine carriages, now preserved from wind and weather at Belton House, near Grantham in Lincolnshire. Owned by the National Trust, this noble 17th-century mansion was home to generations of the Brownlow and Cust families, and is set in a splendid park.*

Opposite page *Fishing for trout in Rutland Water, Leicestershire, one of the biggest man-made lakes in Europe. It covers more than 3,000 acres (1,215 hectares) with a shoreline 24 miles (39km) long. The lake attracts many waterfowl.*

Above *A landmark for miles around, Lincoln Cathedral dominates the city from its high, steep hill. It was rebuilt in the late 12th and 13th centuries after an earthquake in 1185. In the huge central tower, 270ft (82m) high, hangs the massive bell called Great Tom of Lincoln, weighing 5$^{1}/_{2}$ tons.*

Right *Tower Bridge over the Thames, seen from the downstream side, near St Katharine's Dock. The giant steel sundial in the foreground was placed here in 1973. The two leaves of the bridge's roadway rise to let ships through. The bridge was formally opened in 1894.*

Left *Stretching along the Thames by Westminster Bridge, the Houses of Parliament were rebuilt in the Gothic style after a disastrous fire in 1834. The clock tower is prominent at the bridge end of the building. It stands on the site of the old Palace of Westminster, for centuries the principal London residence of the monarch.*

Above *The west front of Buckingham Palace. In the foreground is the monument to Queen Victoria at the end of the Mall, crowned by a golden statue of Victory. George IV and his architect John Nash began to transform Buckingham House into a palace worthy of royalty during the 1820s, but the first sovereign to live there was Queen Victoria. She moved in soon after her accession in 1837.*

Left *The Household Cavalry in their winter uniforms in the Mall. Already a 'grand walk' in the 18th century, the Mall was turned into a processional way between Buckingham Palace and Whitehall in 1910. The first sovereign to proceed along it in state was George V, on the way to his coronation the following year.*

Left *The Harrod family ran a small and undistinguished grocer's shop in what was then the village of Knightsbridge in the 1850s. The redoubtable Charles Digby Harrod began the rapid expansion which turned Harrods into Britain's most famous and fashionable shop, selling virtually everything. The present terracotta building dates from 1905.*

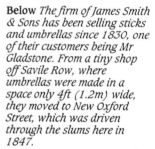

Below *The firm of James Smith & Sons has been selling sticks and umbrellas since 1830, one of their customers being Mr Gladstone. From a tiny shop off Savile Row, where umbrellas were made in a space only 4ft (1.2m) wide, they moved to New Oxford Street, which was driven through the slums here in 1847.*

81

Left *Opening off Piccadilly, the charming Burlington Arcade of smart little shops was completed in 1819. It has been altered several times since, and the south entrance was redesigned in 1931. The uniformed beadles, there to keep order, once had to be former soldiers of the Tenth Hussars, but this rule has been relaxed.*

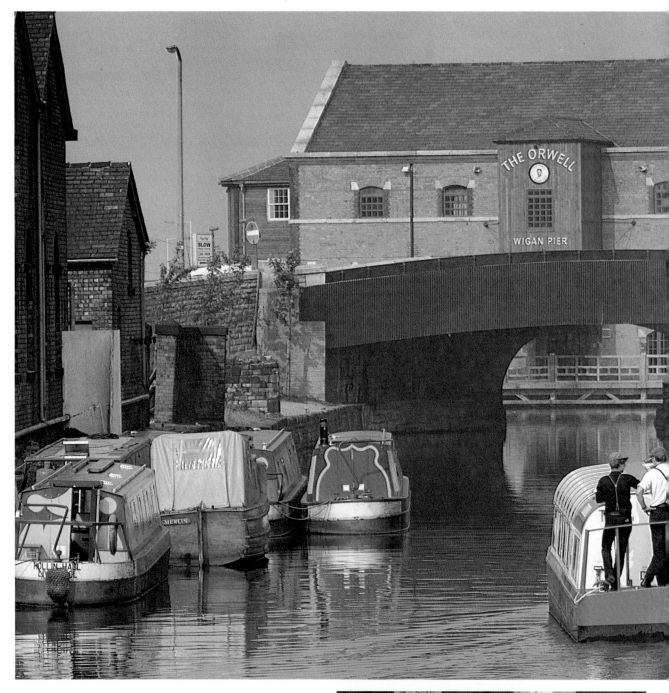

Right *The largest working mill steam engine in the world, in the restored Trencherfield Cotton Mill at the pier in Wigan. Rated at 2,500hp, the engine has a flywheel weighing 70 tons.*

Left *Once a music-hall joke, and subject of jibes by George Formby Senior, Wigan Pier has become a reality and an effective tourist attraction as a 'living history' experience, where visitors step back into the world of 1900. The handsome red brick warehouses have been refurbished and canal boats cruise along the Leeds and Liverpool Canal.*

Right *Statues of Victorian worthies grace Albert Square, outside the Town Hall in the heart of Manchester. In the background is the Prince Consort under his stone canopy. Designed in 1862, before the similar monument in London, this was the first important Albert Memorial in the country.*

Left *The interior of the Roman Catholic cathedral of Christ the King, in Liverpool, is a vast circular space with the high altar in the centre. Above the altar is a modernistic canopy, and high above that again is a lantern with stained glass designed by John Piper and Patrick Reyntiens. The building was designed by Sir Frederick Gibberd and completed in 1967.*

Left *Liverpool's great days as a port are over, but the three striking buildings along the Pierhead are still a symbol of the city's power and pride. In the foreground, seen from the Maritime Museum, is the Dock Board Office of 1907. Behind it is the former Cunard Building of 1906, and behind this again are the high towers of the Royal Liver Building of 1910, topped by the figures of the legendary liver birds that are supposed to have given the city its name.*

86

Above *The two-storeyed, half-timbered, cottage-like building is the porch of the church of St John the Baptist at Berkswell, near Coventry. An outer stair leads to the upper floor. The chancel of the church is Norman.*

Above *Blazing flowerbeds set off the grey stone walls of ruined Dudley Castle. The 14th-century fortress stands on a steep hill, fortified soon after the Norman conquest. There is a zoo in the grounds today, and a chairlift helps visitors to cope with the gradients.*

Overleaf *The windmill at Cley next the Sea has a comparatively unusual conical cap. This north Norfolk village is no longer 'next' the sea, though it was once. Silt has built up along the shore and Cley is now more than a mile (1.6km) inland.*

Left *The handsome Custom House at King's Lynn, built in 1683. Standing on the Great Ouse, not far inland from the Wash, the town was a flourishing port for centuries, because of its excellent river connections with Norfolk, the fen country to the west and north, and the East Midlands area.*

Above *Boats on Horsey Mere, a lake owned by the National Trust, lying close to the sea between Hickling Broad and the coast. Marsh plants, insects and birds flourish here. The Mere is closer to the sea than the other Norfolk Broads, and the water is saltier.*

Above *Village sign at Swanton Morley, near Dereham. In 1615 Richard Lincoln, who lived here, made a will which disinherited his son and caused his descendants to emigrate to the New World. The eventual consequence was that Abraham Lincoln was born in the United States of America instead of England. The remains of the ancestral Lincoln house are now part of the Angel Inn.*

Left *Bowls on the sea front at Hunstanton, Norfolk. The town is at the mouth of the Wash, and this is the only seaside resort on Britain's east coast where you can see the sun set over the sea. It was developed as a resort in the 19th century by the Le Strange family, local landowners, who hold the dignity of Lords High Admiral of the Wash.*

Right *In the church at Burnham Thorpe in Norfolk is the font in which the future Lord Nelson was christened in 1758. There is also a lectern and cross made from the wood of HMS* Victory. *The hero's father, The Rev. Edmund Nelson, was the parson here and is buried in the church. The local pubs are called* The Victory, The Hero *and so on.*

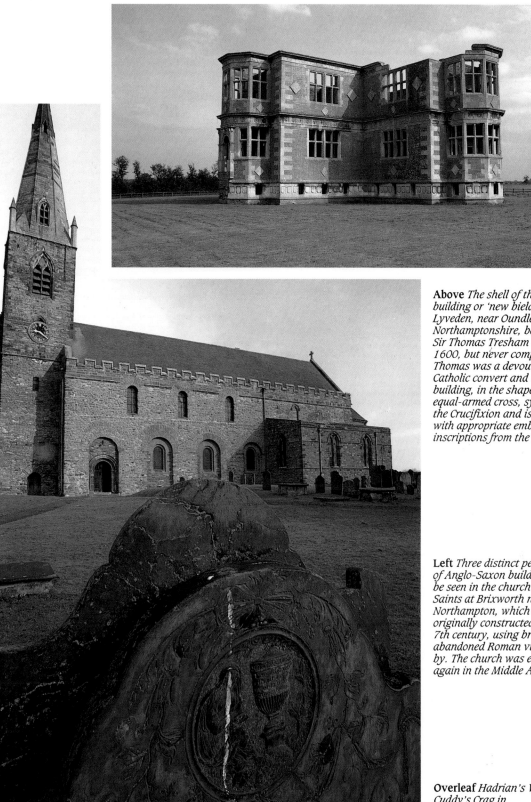

Above *The shell of the new building or 'new bield' at Lyveden, near Oundle in Northamptonshire, begun by Sir Thomas Tresham about 1600, but never completed. Sir Thomas was a devout Roman Catholic convert and the building, in the shape of an equal-armed cross, symbolises the Crucifixion and is adorned with appropriate emblems and inscriptions from the Bible.*

Left *Three distinct periods of Anglo-Saxon building can be seen in the church of All Saints at Brixworth near Northampton, which was originally constructed in the 7th century, using bricks from abandoned Roman villas close by. The church was enlarged again in the Middle Ages.*

93

Overleaf *Hadrian's Wall at Cuddy's Crag in Northumberland. This tremendous fortification, the most impressive object left from the Roman period in Britain, originally stretched for about 73 miles (117km), stood 20ft (6m) high and required a garrison of some 13,000 men. A barrier against the Picts and Scots, it marked the northern frontier of the Roman Empire.*

Left *Tranquillity in the Bolam Lake Country Park. This is a good spot for birdwatching, as great spotted woodpeckers and nuthatches are seen here, and red squirrels as well. The artificial lake was laid out in the early 19th century by John Dobson, the distinguished Newcastle architect.*

Left *High on its crag, Lindisfarne Castle was built about 1550 for the protection of Holy Island against Scottish raiding. It fell into ruin in the 19th century and in 1903 was romantically rebuilt by Edwin Lutyens for Edward Hudson, the publishing magnate who founded* Country Life. *It is now owned by the National Trust.*

Right *Impressive Victorian fireplace in the library of Thoresby Hall, a great house in the Dukeries area of Nottinghamshire. Originally designed by John Carr of York, it was rebuilt on a lavish scale in the 1860s by Anthony Salvin for the wealthy third Earl Manvers.*

Right *The regatta course at Henley-on-Thames, Oxfordshire, in July. One of the major sporting and social occasions of the fashionable year, the regatta began in 1839 and is now the country's most prestigious rowing event.*

Right *'In the spring,' Tennyson wrote, 'a livelier iris changes on the burnished dove.' Here on the roof of Farringdon House the doves are changed into many colours.*

Left *Set on the bank of the Thames in Oxfordshire, Mapledurham House was built in red brick in the time of Elizabeth I for Sir Richard Blount, whose descendants have lived there ever since. The house was considerably altered in the 1790s and again in the 1830s.*

Left *A flotilla of punts on the River Cherwell at Magdalen Bridge, Oxford, which was built in 1782 and widened a hundred years later. The Cherwell joins the Isis (as the Thames is called here) a little way downstream. Punting is one of the great summer pleasures of Oxford.*

Above *Morris dancer and friend on May Day in Oxford. The dancers join the celebrations on the first morning of May every year, when a choir hails the dawn with a hymn in Latin from the top of Magdalen Tower. How this custom began, no one knows, but it apparently goes back to the 16th century.*

Right *Robed academics and dignitaries walk in procession at a ceremony for the conferring of honorary degrees. Oxford University has about 10,000 to 11,000 students at any one time. According to legend, it was founded by Alfred the Great, but students actually started to gather here in the 12th century, after foreign students had been expelled from the University of Paris.*

Below *The clock, with jacks which strike the quarters, is on Carfax Tower. There is a fine view of the city from the top of the 13th-century tower, which is all that is left of the church of St Martin at the head of the High Street. The spot where four streets meet – Carfax is a corruption of the French for 'four ways' – is the centre of Oxford.*

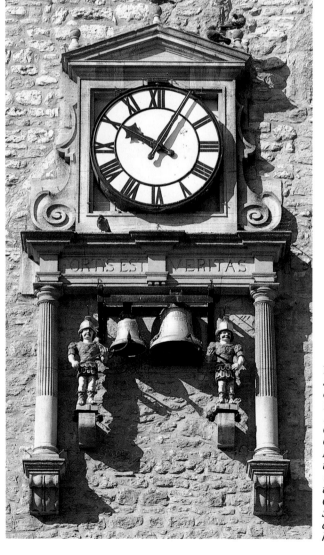

Right *The 'city of dreaming spires' and 'home of lost causes', seen from Boar's Hill. The dome belongs to the 18th-century Radcliffe Camera, designed by James Gibbs, now an extension of the Bodleian Library. The spire to its right, rising to 188ft (57m) is that of St Mary's, the university church. The future Cardinal Newman was vicar of St Mary's from 1828 to 1843, and many famous preachers have graced its pulpit.*

Overleaf *Detail from a stained-glass window by Edward Burne-Jones and William Morris in Holy Trinity Church, Meole Brace, Shropshire. The church, on the outskirts of Shrewsbury, contains magnificent Pre-Raphaelite glass, including windows designed by Ford Madox Brown, and a window by Charles Kempe. The church also has links with the novelist Mary Webb.*

Left *Tinkering with the wheels on the East Somerset Railway at Cranmore, near Shepton Mallet. This delightful preserved steam railway was founded by the artist David Shepherd. Here there are nostalgic steam-train rides, plenty of locomotives and rolling stock to admire, and an art gallery in the signal box.*

Above *Glastonbury Tor in Somerset, crowned by the tower which is all that remains of the church of St Michael. This is probably a sacred place of great antiquity and the lines on the side of the hill may mark the route of a winding spiral path up to the summit, used in pagan rituals long before the coming of Christianity.*

Above *Looking out from the gaping mouth of Thor's Cave in the side of a crag high above the River Manifold, near Wetton in the Staffordshire part of the Peak District. The cave was inhabited in prehistoric times and during the Celtic, Roman and Anglo-Saxon periods. From the outside the entrance looks like a railway arch, though it is, in fact, entirely natural.*

Right *Interior of Christ Church Mansion, at Ipswich in Suffolk. This stately 16th-century house is now a museum of local bygones, pictures, furniture, clocks, tapestries and ceramics. There are works by Constable, Gainsborough, Munnings, and other Suffolk artists.*

Above *The portable desk used by the great man of English literature, Dr Samuel Johnson, is preserved with many other mementos at his birthplace in Lichfield, Staffordshire. The house was his father's bookshop and he was born in the room over the shop in 1709.*

Above *Sculpture by Barbara Hepworth acts as an overture to the performances at The Maltings in Snape, in the background. The 19th-century maltings were converted in the 1960s for the annual Aldeburgh Festival of Music, and almost immediately had to be rebuilt after a fire.*

Right *Racing silks worn by jockeys are on display at the lively National Horseracing Museum, which opened in 1983 and is appropriately in Newmarket. The capital of the turf since the time of Charles II, the town is where the august Jockey Club has its headquarters.*

Left *Brightly painted bathing huts stand in a prim line on the beach at Southwold. The town was bombarded by a German naval force during the First World War because of its 18th-century cannon, which faced out over the sea. They had been captured from the Jacobites by the Duke of Cumberland in 1745.*

Overleaf *The unusual mill at Woodbridge is worked by the rising tide, which brings the water to turn the wheel. This means that the mill has to work highly irregular hours. Built in 1793, the mill has recently been restored to working order.*

Above *The drawing-room at Polesden Lacey near Dorking. Here the noted Edwardian hostess, the Hon. Mrs Ronald Greville, entertained everyone fashionable, from the royal family to Indian maharajahs. The gilded carving and the painted ceiling were brought here from an Italian palace and the house, owned by the National Trust since 1942, contains Mrs Greville's enjoyable art collection.*

Right *The oldest working windmill in Britain spreads its sails on Outwood Common, south-east of Redhill. It was built in 1665 and it is said that in the following year the Great Fire of London could be seen from the top of it. The mill was restored in 1952.*

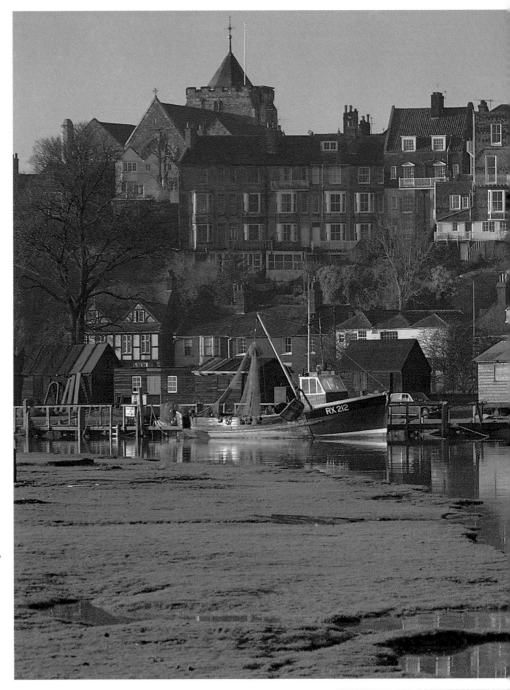

Right *The charming old town of Rye is perched high on a hill above the River Rother, which runs on down to the English Channel. The town was one of the Cinque Ports in medieval times but has been left high and dry, 2 miles (3.2km) inland, by the retreating sea. The church of St Mary has one of the oldest clocks in England, made at Winchelsea in 1561.*

118

Right *The River Cuckmere loops and snakes through the flat country beneath the South Downs on its way towards the sea at Cuckmere Haven, west of Eastbourne. The river rises not far to the north, near Heathfield, and makes its way south through a gap in the Downs at Alfriston.*

Overleaf, left *The white chalk bastion of Beachy Head, near Eastbourne, commands superb views along the Channel coast, towards the Isle of Wight in one direction and Romney Marsh in the other. The red-and-white lighthouse at its foot was built in 1902.*

Overleaf, right *A whirring of wings around the dovecote at Nymans, a masterpiece of a garden at Handcross. The garden was created by the Messel family from 1890 onwards, and passed to the National Trust in the 1950s. There are many rare plants here, with trees and shrubs from all over the world.*

Right *Brass rubbing in the cloisters of Chichester Cathedral. Originally a Norman church, rebuilt many times, the Cathedral is noted for its extensive display of modern art by Graham Sutherland, John Piper and others. It is the only English cathedral with a detached bell tower.*

Below *At the foot of the South Downs, below Chanctonbury Ring, is Wiston Park. Built by Sir Thomas Shirley in Elizabethan times, it was drastically remodelled in the 1830s. The 14th-century church of St Mary, whose plain tower rises beyond the house, has also been extensively restored.*

Opposite *The simple tower of the small village church at Pyecombe, on the South Downs north of Brighton, has a pyramidal roof. The tower dates from the 13th century, while the church is known for its 12th-century lead font and its Jacobean pulpit.*

Right *Newcastle has a splendid handful of bridges over the River Tyne. The most prominent in this picture is the 1928 suspension bridge, with its high curving arch, which carries the Great North Road into the city. Beyond it are the Swing Bridge of 1876, and Robert Stephenson's double-decker High Level Bridge of 1849, carrying the railway on the upper deck and a road on the lower.*

Below *Carved bosses on the ceiling of the 15th-century Percy Chantry, at the east end of Tynemouth Priory. The gaunt ruined shell of the Priory stands impressively on a cliff at the mouth of the River Tyne. The Chantry was restored by the noted 19th-century architect, John Dobson.*

Overleaf *The old-fashioned garden at Anne Hathaway's Cottage at Shottery, outside Stratford-upon-Avon in Warwickshire. The half-timbered house with its thatched roof was the birthplace of Shakespeare's wife. They were married in 1582 and had three children. The cottage belongs to Shakespeare's Birthplace Trust, and is open to the public.*

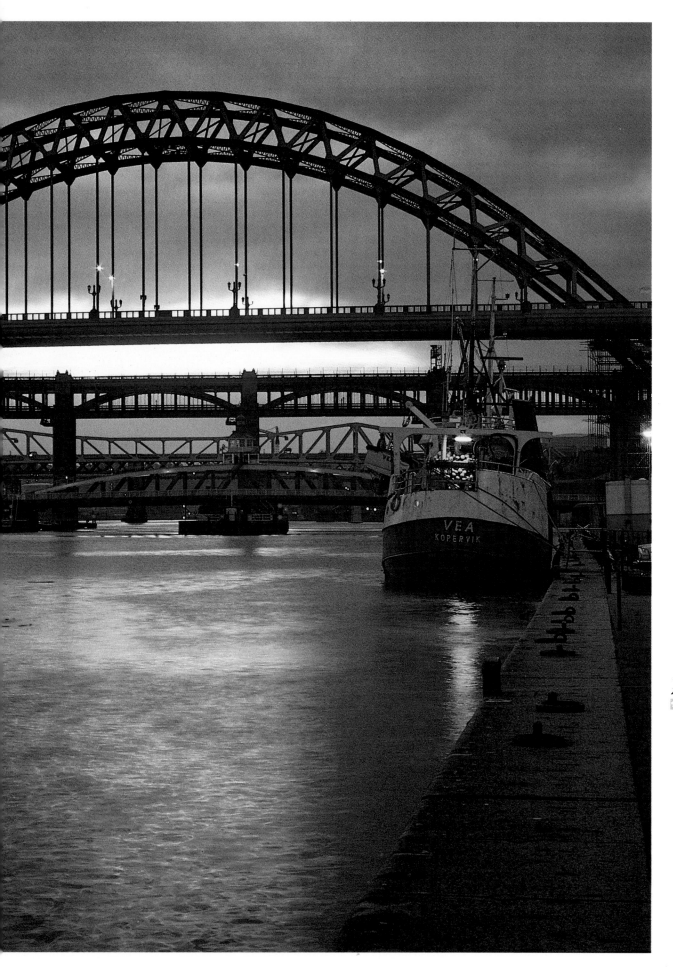

126

Right *Now cared for by the National Trust, the magically beautiful pleasure gardens at Stourhead were created by the Hoare family, wealthy London bankers, in the 18th century. An artificial lake was made by damming the Stour, an elegant bridge constructed, trees planted and classical temples built on the banks and hillside to provide a succession of entrancing vistas.*

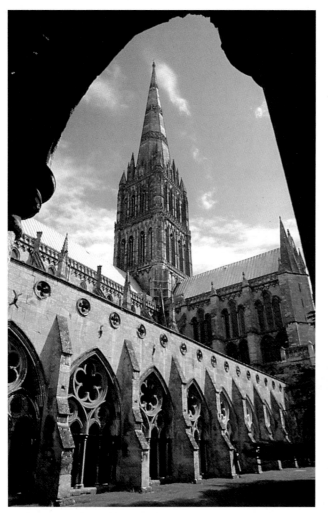

Above *The spire of Salisbury Cathedral, seen from the cloisters. The church was built with remarkable rapidity, in less than 40 years after 1220. The cloisters date from about 1270 and the graceful spire, the highest in England at 404ft (123m), was added in about 1320.*

Overleaf *The most famous prehistoric monument in Britain, Stonehenge was constructed in successive phases over about 1,500 years, starting some 5,000 years ago. Some of the stones were brought laboriously from the Prescelly Hills in south-west Wales, and later the massive sarsen stones, which weigh up to 50 tons apiece, were dragged across country from the downland to the north.*

132

Above *An artist's eye view of Wharfedale, from above the village of Kettlewell, which is on the Dales Way long-distance footpath. Running from Bolton Abbey up to Grassington, Kettlewell and Buckden, Wharfedale is for many visitors the favourite of all the dales.*

Above *Sycamore trees on the slopes of Wensleydale, near Hawes. Known for its gentle, pastoral landscape, the dale has given its name to a mild, whitish cheese. Unlike the other dales, it is not named after the river (the Ure) which runs through it.*

Left *Sheep being auctioned at Hawes, the market town of Upper Wensleydale, which has had a flourishing livestock market for centuries. Wensleydale cheese was originally made from sheep's milk by the monks of Jervaulx Abbey.*

Right *Set some way from its village, the church of St Oswald, Lythe, was built in 1910 on the site of a medieval church. The architect was Sir Walter Tapper. The building commands splendid views over the North Sea, and there are numerous Anglo-Saxon carvings inside.*

136

Above *The Hole of Horcum is a huge natural basin in the North York Moors National Park, north of Levisham. According to legend, it was created by a giant named Wade, who scooped up an enormous handful of earth to throw at his wife. She dodged, and the fistful of soil landed 2 miles (3.2km) away, forming the hill called Blakey Topping.*

Previous page *The scenery of Swaledale in the northern part of the Yorkshire Dales National Park. The Yorkshire Dales National Park was designated in 1954, and is the third-largest national park (after the Lake District and Snowdonia). Swaledale is one of the wilder of these delightful valleys.*

Right *Looking north towards Moorsholm and Commondale, from near Castleton in the North York Moors National Park. The Park was designated in 1952, and covers a remote and comparatively little-visited area of high rolling moors and gentle dales.*

Left *Typical North York Moors pastoral scenery. The Cistercian monks who settled these lonely moorlands kept huge flocks of sheep. The abbey of Rievaulx, for instance, pastured 14,000 sheep on surrounding hills. Sheep farming is still the most important economic activity of the area today.*

139

Left *Observing the action at the cattle auction in Malton. This town, in the old North Riding of Yorkshire, was once the site of a Roman fort, but today it is the setting for one of the most important livestock markets in the North.*

Overleaf, right *The figures which strike the hours and quarters, in a scene from Sir Walter Scott's* Ivanhoe, *are Robin Hood, a swineherd, King Richard the Lionheart and Friar Tuck. The clock is in Thornton's Arcade, which dates from 1878, one of the splendid Victorian shopping arcades in Leeds, West Yorkshire.*

Overleaf, left *The West Beck falls 70ft (21.3m) in Mallyan Spout, a beauty spot near the village of Goathland in the North York Moors National Park.*

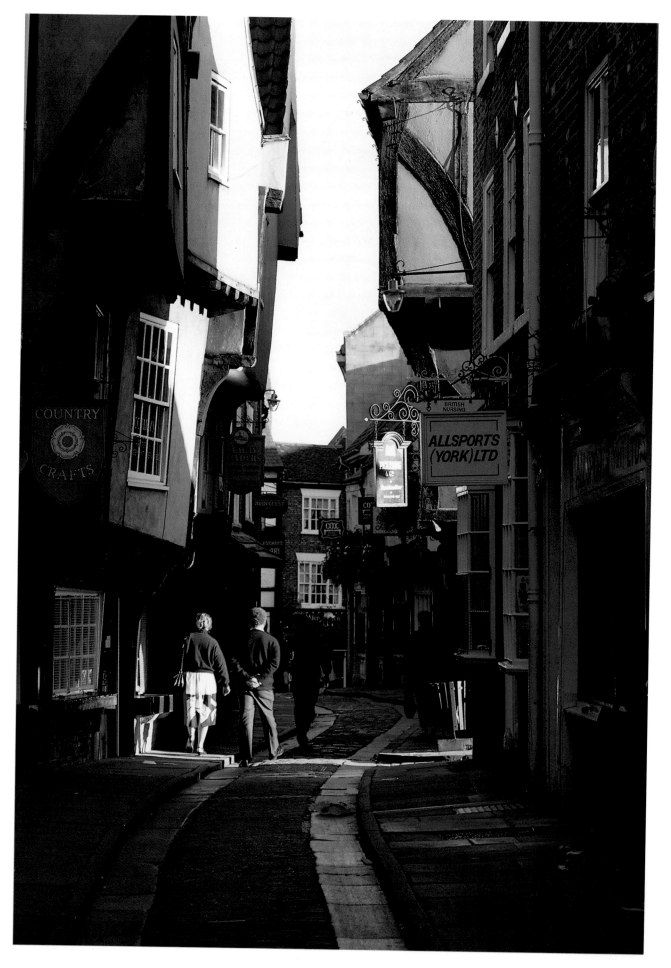

Left *Looking along Low Petergate in York, with the twin west towers of the Minster rising majestically in the background. York was an important Viking town. 'Gate' is from the Danish for 'street'. Much of the city's charm derives from its narrow old streets and 'snickelways', or alleys.*

Below *The National Railway Museum, which moved to York in 1975, has an unrivalled collection, splendidly displayed, with veteran steam locomotives – including the streamlined speedster Mallard – ornate royal carriages, name plates, signs and railway memorabilia of every kind.*

143

Opposite *Some of the oldest buildings in York are the 15th-century houses in the Shambles, which was the street where butchers had their premises from medieval times until the 19th century. Carcasses were hung up on hooks outside the houses, and the street would have reeked of blood and offal.*

SCOTLAND

Previous page *Seen across Loch Scavaig, the 'far Cuillins' of the song rise in snowy splendour on the Isle of Skye. Jagged and precipitous, the Black Cuillins stand in a horseshoe shape around Loch Coruisk, with 20 pointed peaks rising above 3,000ft (914m).*

Below *Smailholm Tower near Kelso is a grim reminder of the time when the Borders area was notoriously dangerous territory, much fought-over and with a long history of raiding and plundering. The tower, whose walls are 7ft (2.1m) thick, was built in the early 1500s. Sir Walter Scott knew it well as a boy.*

146

Above *Testimony to a more peaceful and graceful age, the grand mansion of Mellerstain, north-west of Kelso, was designed by William Adam for the Baillie family in the 1720s and completed by his more famous son, Robert. There are splendid Robert Adam interiors. The gardens were laid out in 1909.*

Right *Sheep and their shepherd in the Border hills near the valley of the River Tweed. In the background is the Talla Reservoir, completed in 1905 to supply water to Edinburgh.*

Previous spread, left *The waterfall at the head of Alva Glen. The valley leads north from the textile town of Alva into the pleasant hill country of the Ochils range. It is also called Silver Glen, because silver was once mined here.*

Previous spread, right *The Balquhidder hills, seen from Strathyre. On the northern outskirts of the beautiful Trossachs region, this area is famed as the haunt of the outlaw Rob Roy MacGregor, who, after a long and glamorously misspent life, was buried in Balquhidder churchyard in 1734.*

Above *Loch Lomond, looking north. Famed for the 'bonnie banks' and 'bonnie braes' of the song, this is the largest expanse of inland water in Britain, 23 miles (37km) long by up to 5 miles (8km) across. In the Middle Ages it was called Loch Leven, but was later renamed after Ben Lomond, the great peak which looms above its eastern flank.*

Right *Steamer trips in the* Sir Walter Scott *are an ideal way to see Loch Katrine, among the mountains of the Trossachs. It was Scott who first sang the praises of this area in his poem* The Lady of the Lake, *published in 1810.*

Right *The 60ft (18m) waterfall called the Grey Mare's Tail, near Dundrennan, is in the area called the Stewartry of Kirkcudbright. This region was controlled by the Maxwell family, hereditary stewards for the kings of Scots. There are two other waterfalls with the same name in Scotland.*

Below *Readying the salmon nets in the long estuary of the River Cree, which rises in the wild country of the Galloway Forest Park and flows southwards through Newton Stewart, past Creetown to the sea. Salmon return to spawn in the river in which they themselves were spawned; many fall victim to the fishermen.*

Overleaf *Looking north towards Hart Fell, from near Moffat, in sheep-farming country among the mountains at the northern end of Annandale. The River Tweed rises in this area, and the Talla Reservoir lies beyond the hills in the distance.*

151

Above *The largest church in all Scotland, the cathedral of St Andrews was reduced to ruins by the puritanical zeal of the Presbyterian reformers in the 16th century, and by the desire of the citizenry for building stone. According to tradition, the bones of St Andrew, Scotland's patron saint, were brought to this site in the 4th century by St Rule. The 108ft (32.9m) tower of the little 12th-century church of St Rule is still standing.*

Overleaf, left *Crathes Castle, east of Banchory in Grampian, reminiscent of a fairytale or a Walt Disney fantasy with its towers and turrets, was built in the 16th century for the Burnett lairds, and combined security against attack with a greater degree of comfort than earlier castles. The last Burnett laird and his wife created the delightful garden, and gave the castle to the National Trust for Scotland.*

Overleaf, right *The harbour and cottages at Pennan, a fishing village on the Buchan coast in Grampian, are tucked in under the high cliffs. Buchan was a Celtic province and later a feudal earldom, which included the low-lying North-East Neuk, or north-eastern knuckle of Scotland, north of Aberdeen. Like Fife, it has retained a certain separate individuality.*

155

Left *The kirk at Moonzie, near Cupar, in the ancient kingdom of Fife. The broad peninsula between the Firth of Tay and the Firth of Forth has always been one of the most prosperous areas in Scotland. It was ruled by its earls, the Macduffs, and has retained its separate identity over the centuries, successfully resisting a bureaucratic attempt to merge it with Tayside in the 1970s.*

Above *Part of the harbour at Anstruther. The town was once the major herring fishing port in Scotland, but today only the Scottish Fisheries Museum recalls the glory of the now depressed fishing industry.*

156

Above *The Laidhay Croft Museum, north of Dunbeath on the Caithness coast, contains the bygones of a crofter's home in the 1930s.*

Previous page *Dunnottar Castle stands grimly on its isolated rock south of Stonehaven, Grampian. The keep was built in the 14th century. This was the fastness of the Keith family, hereditary Earls Marshall of Scotland, and it was here that royal regalia of Scotland were kept during the Civil War. The Keiths forfeited the castle when the 10th Earl joined the Jacobite rising of 1715, and the fortress fell into ruins.*

Right *Silver skean dhu, or dagger, and sporran, in the Inverness Museum, which has an important collection of Highland silver and displays on the life of Highland clans. A sporran is a large purse or pouch, made from the skin of an animal, usually with the hair left on.*

Opposite *The mighty hump of Slioch, garlanded with clouds, towers up a sheer 3,217ft (981m) on the northern side of Loch Maree in Wester Ross. The Loch, with its islands, is a particularly beautiful stretch of water in a region of scenic grandeur.*

162

164

Opposite *The Falls of Measach near Braemore tumble 150ft (45.7m) into the deep Corrieshalloch Gorge, a geological fault in the landscape about 1 mile (1.6km) long. A suspension bridge provides a good view of the gorge and the falls.*

Below *The village of Plockton was founded late in the 18th century as a fishing settlement for Highlanders driven from the land in the Clearances, to make way for sheep. It is now a centre for sailing and water-sports. In the background lies Loch Carron, cradled among the mountains.*

Previous page *On the southern side of Loch Maree are the great peaks of Beinn Eighe, 3,309ft (1,008m) and Liathach, 3,456ft (1,053m), seen here from Loch Clair, at the eastern end of Glen Torridon. The first National Nature Reserve in Britain was constituted here in 1951.*

Above *Rock stacks at Duncansby Head, at the north-eastern corner of mainland Scotland and the eastern entrance to the Pentland Firth. The sea carved these arches from the cliffs. Ptolemy located this headland on his world map in the 2nd century AD.*

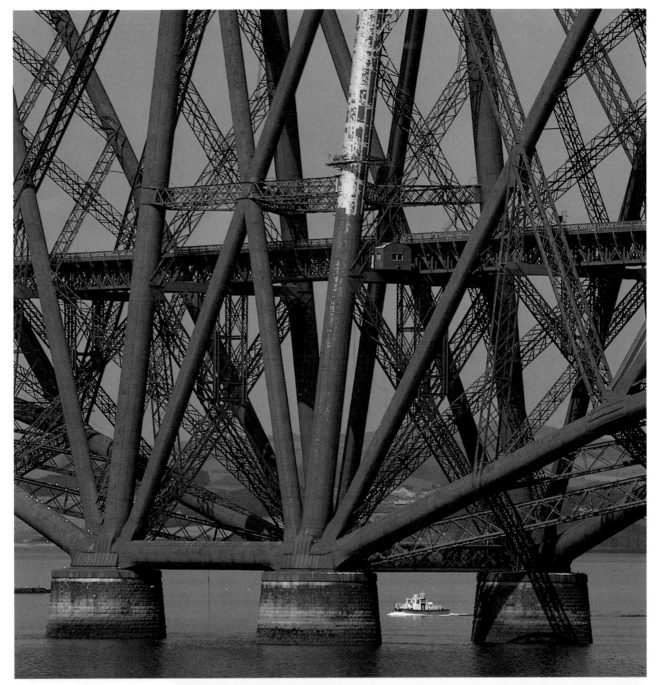

Above *Part of the giant cantilevered Forth Railway Bridge in Lothian, formally opened in 1890 by the Prince of Wales (the future Edward VII).*

Right *Preston Mill at East Linton in Lothian, which dates from the 16th century.*

Left *The Pass of Glencoe, Highland, under an ominous sky. It is famed for the massacre perpetrated here on a winter's night in 1692, and for the magnificence of its mountain scenery. Much of the land here is owned by the National Trust for Scotland.*

Right *An exploding galaxy of blazing rockets lights the sky above central Edinburgh. Fireworks celebrate the Edinburgh International Festival in August every year. Britain's most celebrated arts festival began in 1947, and includes a spectacular military tattoo at the castle.*

Above *Figures on an ornamental fountain contrast with the austere, barracks-like simplicity and strength of Edinburgh Castle on its rock high above the city. The Castle has been a fortified refuge since prehistoric times. The town grew up beneath the rock's protection, and became the capital city of Scotland under the Stuart dynasty in the 15th century.*

169

Above *Tulips make a carpet of honour leading to the monument to Sir Walter Scott in the gardens beside Princes Street. The statue has become one of Edinburgh's best-known landmarks since the foundation stone was laid in 1840. Beneath the Gothic canopy is a statue by Thomas Steell of Sir Walter with his favourite dog, Maida.*

Left *The library of the Glasgow School of Art. Designed by the city's most famous architect, Charles Rennie Mackintosh, this is one of the most celebrated of Glasgow's many fine buildings. It was built between 1897 and 1909.*

Overleaf, left *Glen Croe, among the mountains of the Argyll Forest Park. This area on the Cowal Peninsula, between the Firth of Clyde and Loch Fyne, was long dominated by the Campbell clan. It was the first forest park designated by the Forestry Commission in the 1930s.*

Overleaf, right *Inverary Castle, home of the Duke of Argyll, chief of the Clan Campbell. The Castle was rebuilt in the mid-18th century in a Palladian-Gothic style. The pointed caps on the towers are Victorian.*

Below *Cranes in the shipyards. Glasgow was a major shipbuilding centre from the 19th century until the years after the Second World War.*

Left *The grand staircase of Pollok House, an 18th-century Palladian mansion designed by William Adams, which was enlarged and altered in about 1900. It belonged to the Maxwell family. Now a museum, it contains a distinguished collection of pictures, including works by El Greco, Murillo and Goya.*

Opposite *Stair rises upon stair inside the imposing City Chambers, or Town Hall. Rich in marble, majolica and mosaics, it was completed in 1889, a monument to Glasgow's Victorian opulence and civic pride.*

172

Left *The ruins of Ardchonnel Castle, a 15th-century Campbell stronghold on a small island in Loch Awe. The Loch, 22 miles (35.2km) long and about 1 mile (1.6km) across, is one of Scotland's largest natural stretches of water and acted as a moat protecting the Campbell territory in Argyll. The clan liked to boast of the inaccessibility of their heartland.*

Below *Throwing the hammer at the Highland Games in Pitlochry. These traditional contests have their origins in the war training of the Highland clans, but they became popular as sporting and romantic spectacles in the 19th century, and are now important tourist attractions.*

175

Overleaf *Sheep graze peacefully beside Loch Tay, while across the water Ben Lawers raises its mighty head to 3,984ft (1,214m). The National Nature Reserve here is renowned for its Alpine and Arctic plants. There are red deer, too, and golden eagles are sometimes seen.*

180

Right *Placid white-washed cottages on the Vaternish Peninsula of Skye, the largest of the Hebridean islands. Skye was ruled by the Norse until 1263, when the Norse were defeated at the Battle of Largs and the Hebrides were ceded to the kingdom of Scotland.*

Previous spread, left *Loch Tummel near Pitlochry, towards the formidable hump of Schiehallion, 'the fairy hill'.*

Previous spread, right *Glamis Castle in its Scots baronial majesty is the seat of the Earls of Strathmore and was the family home of Queen Elizabeth the Queen Mother.*

Above *Castle Moil's fangs guard Kyleakin at the shortest crossing point between Skye and the mainland, at Kyle of Lochalsh. The crossing is only a few hundred yards over the water, through which King Haakon of Norway sailed on his way to defeat at the Battle of Largs.*

Right *'Over the sea to Skye': the misty coastline of the island which has a romantic place in history because of its role in the events of 1746, when Charles Edward Stuart, the 'Young Pretender', was hunted through the Highlands after his defeat at Culloden. It was to Skye that the Prince was taken by Flora Macdonald, disguised as her servant.*

182

Above *A typical scene in the Outer Hebrides, at Loch Maaruig, an inlet on Loch Seaforth in the Isle of Harris. The pile of peat in the foreground is a reminder that peat is the fuel of these remote island settlements, which live principally by fishing and sheep-farming.*

Left *A bundle of tweed left for collection on a gatepost in Harris. Real Harris Tweed is woven by the islanders in their homes, and until the 1930s was still coloured with vegetable dyes made by the locals from heather, lichens and roots. Falling demand and competition from cheaper cloth has put the industry in difficulty in recent years.*

Below *The tiger snarls a feudal greeting at Kinloch Castle on Rum, a Victorian edifice from the days when this island in the Inner Hebrides was a private sporting estate. Red deer were imported in the 19th century for stalking and shooting. The island is now a nature reserve, owned by the Nature Conservancy Council, and the Castle is a hotel.*

183

WALES

Left *The massive round towers, now impotent, of Rhuddlan Castle beside the River Clwyd near Rhyl, were built for Edward I between 1277 and 1282 by the great military engineer, James of St George. It was from Rhuddlan in 1284 that King Edward issued a statute providing for the future government of conquered Wales.*

Right *Pistyll Rhaeadr, in the Berwyn Mountains, is the highest waterfall in Wales. The River Disgynfa drops 240ft (73m) down the precipice here in two leaps. The Welsh name, Pistyll Rhaeadr, literally means 'waterfall waterfall'.*

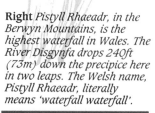

Previous spread *Who built this rough stairway of flat slabs of rock remains a mystery. They are called the Roman Steps, but have also been attributed to ancient Welsh or medieval hands. The steps lie on a packhorse trail in the wild, mountainous country below Rhinog Fawr, 2,362ft (720m).*

Right *The magnificent ornamental gates of Chirk Castle, north of Oswestry, were made in 1721 by the famous Davies Brothers of Bersham, Robert and John, renowned for their ironwork. The heraldry relates to the Myddelton family, who acquired the Castle in 1595 and owned it for nearly 400 years.*

188

Above *The piers of the soaring Pontcysyllte Aqueduct carry the Shropshire Union Canal in an iron trough over the River Dee, 120ft (36.5m) below, east of Llangollen. One of the master works of the great engineer Thomas Telford, the aqueduct was completed in 1805.*

Left *The Boat Inn at the village of Erbistock, in the valley of the Dee south of Wrexham. One of the major rivers of Wales, the Dee flows from Bala Lake eastwards to Llangollen. Near Erbistock it turns north to Chester, on its way to the Irish Sea.*

Left *A miner's safety helmet and other relics in the Chwarel Wynne museum of slate mining at Glyn Ceiriog. The wooded Ceiriog valley lies west of Chirk. Visitors can enjoy underground tours of the mine, as well as a nature trail.*

Left *The medieval walled town of Tenby on the Pembrokeshire coast was converted into an elegant seaside resort in the 19th century, largely by an energetic local landowner, Sir William Paxton. Sailing yachts find shelter in the quay. The ruins of the castle crown Castle Hill in the background. The town was the birthplace of the painter, Augustus John.*

Below *Cenarth Falls on the River Teifi, which is famous for its salmon. Coracles were used by the fishermen here until quite recently, and there are still coracle races every year at Cilgerran.*

191

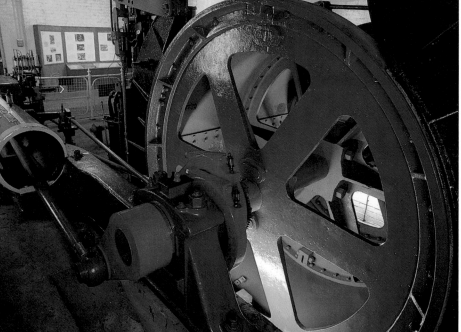

Left *The mound of earth which originally covered the Pentre Ifan burial chamber in the Preseli Hills has worn away over 4,000 years and more, and left the massive stones of this prehistoric tomb exposed. A capstone 16ft (4.8m) long is supported on uprights 7 or 8ft (2.1-2.4m) high.*

Below *The Nant-y-moch reservoir in beautiful country north-east of Aberystwyth is named after a chapel which was drowned when the valley of the Rheidol was dammed here. The dam, completed in 1965, stands 170ft (52m) high and is 1,150ft (350m) long. A minor road from Talybont to Ponterwyd runs close to the reservoir, which lies below the high moorland of Plynlimon.*

Far left *Industrial machinery, locomotives and displays on coal mining in the area can be enjoyed at the Kidwelly Industrial Museum, housed in an old tinplate works.*

Left *A monument of medieval Wales, Carreg Cennen Castle rears up on its lonely rock 300ft (91.4m) above the River Cennen. Dating from about 1300, it was partially destroyed in 1462, because it had become a base for a gang of robbers. According to legend, the Welsh hero Owain Llawgoch sleeps in a cave here, waiting to return when Wales needs him.*

Overleaf *View from one of the lighthouses at Nash Point on the Bristol Channel coast of South Glamorgan. The sandbanks off shore were notoriously dangerous and claimed many seamen's lives in the age of sail.*

Right *Looking like a giant weathered sphinx or prehistoric monster with its bands of rock, Nash Point rises above the Glamorgan shore. It was the loss of 81 lives here in a shipwreck in 1831 that convinced authority of the need for a lighthouse.*

Left *Ruritanian and romantic on its wooded hillside outside Cardiff, Castell Coch has appeared in films like* The Prisoner of Zenda. *It was built in the 19th century, on the ruins of a medieval castle, by the third Marquess of Bute, whose family had made a huge fortune from their development of Cardiff as a coal port. The architect was the brilliantly eccentric William Burges, who had already worked with the Marquess of Bute on Cardiff Castle. Burges created Castell Coch as a hunting lodge.*

Right *The third Marquess of Bute and the architect, William Burges, joined forces to rebuild Cardiff Castle, which they turned into a mock-medieval fortress to surpass all real medieval ones. The interiors are a marvel of outlandish imagination supported by superlative craftsmanship, as in the Arab Room, with its ceiling in gold leaf.*

Left *This unique fortified bridge guards the crossing of the River Monnow at the southern end of the town of Monmouth in Gwent. It was built in the 13th century. This was the county town of the old county of Monmouthshire. Henry V was born here in 1387, and the central square is called Agincourt Square in his honour.*

Below *Pausing for a breather on the Offa's Dyke Path, these hikers enjoy a view over the River Wye. The footpath, one of ten 'national trails', in England and Wales, runs the whole length of the Marches between Chepstow and Prestatyn.*

199

Left *In West Glamorgan, beyond the Gower Peninsula village of Rhossili and the headland, lies Worms Head, so called because of its resemblance to a sea serpent. A blowhole on Worms Head throws up sheets of spray at high tide and makes an eerie booming sound. It is now a nature reserve.*

200

Above *On a rocky shelf above the Wye, Chepstow Castle is one of the oldest stone castles in Europe. The formidable battlements surround the Norman keep, which was erected by William FitzOsbern, one of William the Conqueror's right-hand men.*

Right *View across the sunlit pastures of Gwent to the Black Mountains.*

Opposite *The ruins of Tintern Abbey beside the Wye, seen from the vantage point of the Devil's Pulpit. The Cistercian monastery was founded in the early 12th century, in what was then a wild area of Wales.*

Left *The waterlily canal at Bodnant Garden near Conwy, with the Pin Mill, a garden house of 1730, at the far end. The garden was created from the 1870s onwards by a Lancashire businessman named Henry Pochin and his descendants, assisted by three generations of head gardeners named Puddle. It is now cared for by the National Trust.*

Below *This stained glass window by Rainbow Glass of Beaumaris has recently been installed at the Anglesey Sea Zoo. The enjoyable aquarium near Brynsiencyn in Anglesey specialises in the fish, lobsters, crabs, octopuses, conger eels and other creatures which live in Anglesey waters. The aquarium has touch pools and a tide tank.*

Opposite *The Pont-y-pair, or Bridge of the Cauldron, spans the River Llugwy at Betws-y-Coed, a holiday resort set in wonderful forest and river scenery in the Snowdonia National Park. The bridge is thought to date from the 15th century. The Forestry Commission has waymarked several woodland trails in this area.*

Right *The Lleyn Peninsula protrudes some 25 miles (40km) into the sea at the north-western corner of Wales (*lleyn *in Welsh means peninsula). The coast is an official Area of Outstanding Natural Beauty. There are prehistoric tombs here and churches on the ancient pilgrim route to Bardsey Island. Welsh is the first language.*

Below *Slate quarrying was a major industry in Snowdonia in the 19th century. The workshops of the Dinorwic slate quarry at Llanberis, which closed down at the end of the 1960s, are now home to the Welsh Slate Museum (a branch of the National Museum of Wales). Visitors can see traditional slate crafts being demonstrated.*

Right *A symbol of centuries of English domination, Harlech Castle was built for Edward I by James of St George and completed in 1289 as one of a chain of fortresses to hold Gwynedd in subjection. It stands on a high rock looking out over Cardigan Bay. The song 'Men of Harlech' refers to the Castle's garrison of men, who withstood a siege here for seven years in the 1460s.*

Overleaf *The most impressive of all Edward I's Welsh fortresses was built beside the River Seiont at Caernarvon, the original architect being James of St George. The many-sided towers and the banded masonry imitated the walls of the city of Constantinople, probably because an old tradition identified the Roman fort of Segontium at Caernarvon as the birthplace of the Emperor Constantine the Great. Prince Charles was formally invested as Prince of Wales at the Castle by the Queen in 1969.*

207

208

Above *High mountains and deep valleys draw climbers and walkers to the Snowdonia National Park. Here the black peak of Tryfan is seen beyond the brooding lake of Llyn Idwal. According to legend, no birds will fly over Llyn Idwal's dark water.*

Right *A rack-and-pinion steam railway has been carrying visitors to the summit of Snowdon since 1896.*

Opposite *To the south of Snowdon, the beautiful Nant Gwynant pass connects two lakes, with mountains on either side.*

Right *One of the waterfalls on the River Mellte, to the south of the Brecon Beacons, whose Welsh name means 'river of lightning'. The stream vanishes underground to thunder through caves before emerging to tumble down falls.*

Previous spread *The narrow, boulder-strewn Pass of Llanberis shoulders its way between walls of black rock, where the River Peris struggles through the mountains. The wealth of wildlife in the Snowdonia National Park includes polecats, pine martens and otters, and a great richness of birds and plants.*

213

Left *Lovespoons in the Brecknock Museum in Brecon. It used to be the custom in Wales for a young man to carve a spoon for his sweetheart as a love token. Carved from a single piece of wood, they were sometimes extremely elaborate, and the more complicated and difficult the task, the greater the maker's love. The custom goes back at least to the 16th century.*

Above *Fishing in the Usk Reservoir near Trecastle. This artificial lake, nearly 2 miles (3.2km) long, stores water for Swansea. It lies below Carmarthen Van, 2,632ft (802m), on whose slopes the River Usk rises. From the reservoir the Usk flows eastwards to Brecon and then south-east to Abergavenny, before finally reaching the Bristol Channel.*

Left *Llyn Brianne in the lovely valley of the River Towy on the borders of Dyfed and Powys is a reservoir providing water for Swansea. The lake, which is almost 3 miles (4.8km) long, lies to the west of Llanwrtyd Wells. Not far away is a cave which was used as a hiding place by Twm Shon Catti, 'the Robin Hood of Wales'.*

Above *Water cascades down the 120ft (36.5m) dam of the Craig Goch Reservoir. This is the most northerly of four artificial lakes near Rhayader. They were created between 1892 and 1906, when the valley was flooded to provide water for Birmingham. The Claerwen Reservoir to the south-west was added in 1952. The reservoirs have become an important tourist attraction.*

Left *A lock on the Monnow Brec Canal. This was once two waterways, the Monmouthshire Canal and the Abergavenny Canal, which joined in 1812. The Canal carried iron ore, coal and limestone to the South Wales industrial areas, and then took goods on down to Newport for export.*

Right *Interior of Tretower Court, an unusually well-preserved late medieval manor house, now in the charge of CADW (Welsh Historic Monuments). The house belonged to the Vaughan family, one of whom was the 17th-century metaphysical poet Henry Vaughan.*

Above *Looking from darkness into light through a window of Bronllys Castle, north-west of Talgarth, a round tower dating from about 1200, built on an earlier mound.*

Left *Seen in the distance are the Black Mountains, whose highest peak is Waun Fach, 2,660ft (811m), east of Brecon. The range looks black, though it is actually composed of red sandstone. There is delightful walking country here on the long hill ridges, and a chance of seeing the rare red kite.*

Previous spread *Abergwesyn Pass in the delectable valley of the River Irfon, in the remote Powys countryside north-west of Llanwrtyd Wells. The river rises near the Claerwen Reservoir further north. It flows through Llanwrtyd Wells and on to join the Wye outside Builth Wells.*

Below *'Sheep may safely graze...': a tranquil scene on the River Usk. In the background is Pen y Fan, 2,907ft (886m). It is the highest peak in the Brecon Beacons range, and the highest in Britain south of Snowdonia. The National Park was established in 1957 and covers an area of 519 square miles (1,344 square km).*

220

Above *View of the Brecon Beacons from Pen-y-crug, a high point north-west of Brecon. The sandstone mountains were formed some 400 million years ago, and their slopes were dramatically carved by ice-age glaciers. Ravens and buzzards are common here.*

FINIS

INDEX